OUR FATHER WH

HALLOWED

THY KING

THY WILL BE DONE IN E

GIVE US THIS DAY

AND FORGIVE

AS WE FORGIVE

AND LEAD US NOT

BUT DELIVER

FOR THINE IS

AND THE POWER,

FOR EVE

Overcoming Your Inner Barriers
to Intimacy with God

SOMETIMES IT'S HARD TO LOVE GOD.

Dennis Guernsey

InterVarsity Press is the book-publishing division of Inter-Varsity Christian Fellowship, a student movement active on campus at hundreds of universities, colleges and schools of nursing. For information about local and regional activities, write Public Relations Dept., InterVarsity Christian Fellowship, 6400 Schroeder Rd., P.O. Box 7895, Madison, WI 53707-7895.

Distributed in Canada through InterVarsity Press, 860 Denison St., Unit 3, Markham, Ontario L3R 4H1, Canada.

All Scripture quotations, unless otherwise indicated, are from the Holy Bible, New International Version. Copyright © 1973, 1978, International Bible Society. Used by permission of Zondervan Bible Publishers.

Quotations from the Lord's Prayer are from the King James (Authorized) Version.

"The Death of the Hired Man," by Robert Frost. Copyright 1930 by Holt, Rinehart and Winston and renewed 1958 by Robert Frost. Reprinted from The Poetry of Robert Frost, edited by Edward Connery Lathem by permission of Henry Holt and Company, Inc.

ISBN 0-8308-1257-1

Printed in the United States of America.

Library of Congress Cataloging-in-Publication Data

Guernsey, Dennis B.
    Sometimes it's hard to love God: overcoming your inner barriers
to intimacy with God/Dennis Guernsey.
        p.   cm.
    ISBN 0-8308-1257-1
    1. God—Worship and love.   2. Lord's prayer.   I. Title.
BV4817.G813   1989
242'.722—dc20   89-15306
                                                        CIP

16   15   14   13   12   11   10   9   8   7   6   5   4   3   2   1
99   98   97   96   95   94   93   92   91   90   89